cloverleaf books™

Planet Protectors

Rally For Recycling

Lisa Bullard

illustrated by **Wes Thomas**

M MILLBROOK PRESS · MINNEAPOLIS

For Anne —L.B.
For Mom, Dad, Susan, and Ben —W.T.

Millbrook Press
A division of Lerner Publishing Group, Inc.
241 First Avenue North
Minneapolis, MN 55401 U.S.A.

Website address: www.lernerbooks.com

Main body text set in Slappy Inline. Typeface provided by T26.

Library of Congress Cataloging-in-Publication Data
Bullard, Lisa.
    Rally for recycling / by Lisa Bullard ; illustrated by Wes Thomas.
        p.   cm. — (Cloverleaf books. Planet protectors)
    Includes index.
    ISBN 978-0-7613-6103-9 (lib. bdg. : alk. paper)
    1. Refuse and refuse disposal—Juvenile literature. 2. Recycling (Waste, etc.)—
Juvenile literature. I. Thomas, Wes, ill. II. Title.
    TD792.B85 2012
    363.72'82—dc22   2010051509

Manufactured in the United States of America
1 – BP – 7/15/11

TABLE OF CONTENTS

Chapter One

Too Much Trash

Some kids want to be firefighters.

Some kids want to be teachers.

My name's Tyler. Guess what?

I'm going to be an Earth saver when I grow up.

But maybe I shouldn't wait. People are **making** an awful lot of **trash.**

I better take charge before it's too late!

People in the United States are big trash makers. Each person makes more than 4 pounds (1.8 kilograms) of trash each day. Some of this trash is burned. But this makes the air dirty. Some of this trash is buried. But buried trash can last hundreds of years. And it takes up lots of space.

Chapter Two

Recycling Helps Clean Up

Mom says it's great that I want to clean up the Earth. But she wants me to start with my room.

Look at it. It's not that bad, is it?

9

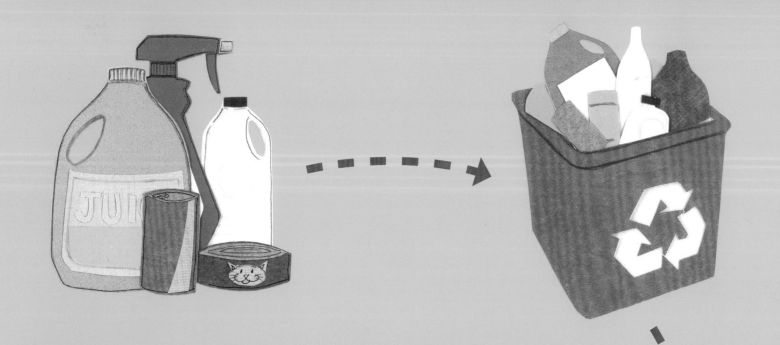

Cleaning my room makes more trash. It's a good thing my teacher explained about recycling. **Recycling** means changing something we don't need into **something we can use.**

Do you think I could **recycle** my sister?

Maybe into a lizard?

Dad says no about the lizard idea. But I can recycle these plastic bottles. And these cans and magazines too.

CANS

PAPER

PLASTIC

Then they won't end up in the **trash.**

We can also recycle glass jars, newspapers, and cardboard. Some of these things have the recycling mark on them. It looks like this:

GLASS

Chapter Three

Sorting It All Out

I'm pretty thirsty after carrying the recycling outside. I'll get a drink from the faucet. That way I won't empty another bottle.

It's good to recycle. But it's even better to make less trash. Avoid plastic water bottles when you can. Fill a cup instead.

Guess where my dog, Pete, drinks from?

People in a big truck will pick up my recycling. They will take it to a **recycling center**.

Workers will sort it into groups. They put cans with cans. They put paper with paper.

Some things can be recycled only once. But we can recycle cans many times.

Chapter Four

Surprise!

Companies will buy the recycling. They might use it to make new cans or paper. But sometimes they turn the recycling into something totally different. Companies even make T-shirts out of plastic. Could you be **wearing bottles?**

There are many recycling surprises. Companies make sandals out of old tires. They make chairs out of old cans. They make carpet out of plastic bottles.

This trash problem is going to take some work. Maybe you could help by recycling too?

Buying goods made from recycled things is also important. Look for the recycling mark inside a circle. It means the item has been made from something recycled. Watch for it the next time you go shopping.

Then I can find another way

Electronic Recycling

to save the planet tomorrow.

Recycle a Rainbow Activity

Did you know crayons can be recycled too?
You can make new super crayons at home.

You will need:

old or broken crayons   an oven
an old muffin pan filled with cup liners   a grown-up (to use the oven)

Recycling follows some basic steps. You will follow some of these same steps.
The steps are gathering, cleaning, sorting, and changing.

Step 1: Gathering
Gather all your old and broken color crayons.

Step 2: Cleaning
Clean the crayons by taking off the wrappers. Then break the crayons into
small pieces.

Step 3: Sorting
Sort the crayons into the different cups in the muffin pan. You can use one
cup for each color if you want. You know, blues with blues and reds with reds.
Or you can mix different colors together. Why not recycle a rainbow?

Step 4: Changing
You must have a grown-up for this step! That's because the grown-up needs
to use the oven. It will change the old crayons into new super crayons.
Here are directions for your grown-up:

1) Preheat the oven to about 250°F (120°C).

2) Cook the crayons for about 10 to 20 minutes.
Cooking time will vary. Check every 5 minutes. When
the crayons look melted, remove from oven.

3) Cool the crayons in the muffin pan for 1 hour.

Step 5: It's your turn again!
Remove the super crayons from the liners. Then
have fun! Why not color a poster about recycling
for your home?

burn: to set something on fire

bury: to dig a hole in the ground, put an object in the hole, and cover it with dirt

goods: things that people buy and sell

plastic: something invented by people that can be made into things such as water bottles and toys

recycle: to turn trash into something that people can use

sort: to separate things into groups

trash: things that people throw away. Trash is also called garbage.

BOOKS

Inches, Alison. *The Adventures of a Plastic Bottle: A Story about Recycling.* New York: Little Simon, 2009. This book tells the story of a plastic bottle that is recycled into a fleece jacket.

Pohl, Kathleen. *What Happens at a Recycling Center*. Strongsville, OH: Gareth Stevens Publishing, 2007. Follow along with Buddy Bear as he takes you on a tour of a recycling center.

WEBSITES

EPA: Recycle City
http://www.epa.gov/recyclecity/
This website is from the Environmental Protection Agency. It lets you explore Recycle City through games and activities.

North Carolina Division of Pollution Prevention and Environmental Assistance: Recycle Guys
http://www.recycleguys.org/
This Recycle Guys website has cartoons and videos. It will help you learn more about recycling.

PBS KIDS GO!: EekoWorld
http://pbskids.org/eekoworld/index.html?load=garbage_recycling
This website from PBS Kids shows you a movie about recycling.

Wisconsin DNR: Environmental Education for Kids
http://www.dnr.state.wi.us/org/caer/ce/eek/earth/recycle/index.htm
This website is from the Wisconsin Department of Natural Resources. It has fun recycling activities and games.